Text and illustrations copyright © 1982 by Kingfisher Books Limited.
All rights reserved including the right of reproduction in
whole or in part in any form.
Published by LITTLE SIMON, a Simon & Schuster Division
of Gulf and Western Corporation. Simon & Schuster Building,
1230 Avenue of the Americas, New York, New York 10020

Printed in Italy by Vallardi Industrie Grafiche, Milan

10 9 8 7 6 5 4 3 2

LITTLE SIMON and colophon are trademarks of Simon & Schuster.

ISBN: 0-671-45045-X
81-20919

LITTLE SIMON

Written and illustrated by Mik Brown

Little Simon
Published by Simon & Schuster, New York

1 one mouse in the rain

one

2

two elephants having a bath

two

3

three crocodiles in canoes

three

four bears on unicycles

4

four

five tigers playing tunes

5

five

six tortoises skipping

6

six

seven birds in airplanes

7

seven

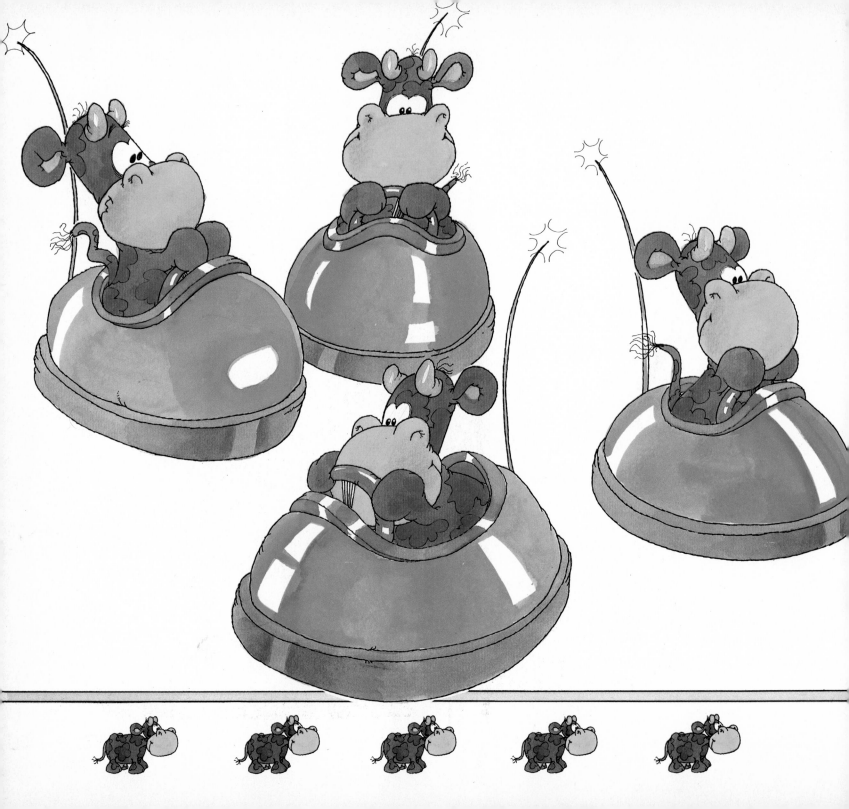

eight cows in bumper cars

8

eight

9

nine puppies playing ball

nine

10

ten monkeys
swinging

ten

Counting Games

Now can you count the animals for yourself?

How many elephants are here?
How many of them are standing?
How many are sitting?

1 elephant and 1 elephant $\xrightarrow{\text{together make}}$ 2 elephants

1 and 1 $\xrightarrow{\text{together make}}$ 2

How many hippos are boxing?
How many hippos are watching?
How many hippos are there all together?

1 hippo and 2 hippos   together make →   3 hippos

1 and 2   together make →   3

How many lions are eating ice cream?
How many lions are not eating ice cream?
How many lions are there all together?

1 lion and 3 lions together make→ 4 lions

1 and 3 together make→ 4

How many giraffes are here?
How many giraffes are wearing bow ties?
How many giraffes are not wearing bow ties?

1 giraffe and 4 giraffes →together make→ 5 giraffes

1 and 4 →together make→ 5

How many frogs are leaping?
How many frogs are sitting still?
How many frogs are there all together?

1 frog and 5 frogs $\xrightarrow{\text{together make}}$ 6 frogs

1 and 5 $\xrightarrow{\text{together make}}$ 6

How many of these leopards have spots?
How many have no spots at all?
How many leopards are there all together?

1 leopard and 6 leopards →together make→ 7 leopards
1 and 6 →together make→ 7

How many snails are not wearing glasses?
How many snails are wearing glasses?
How many snails are there all together?

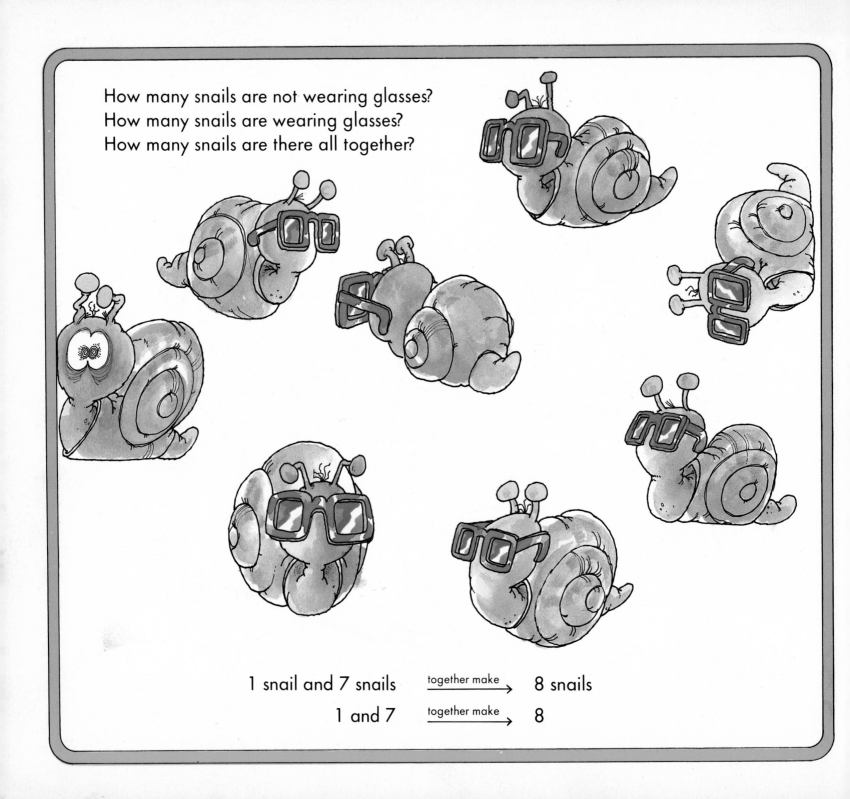

1 snail and 7 snails together make → 8 snails

1 and 7 together make → 8

How many pigs have straight tails?
How many pigs have curly tails?
How many pigs are there all together?

1 pig and 8 pigs   together make →   9 pigs

1 and 8   together make →   9

How many bees are wearing hats?
How many bees are not wearing hats?
How many bees are there all together?
Are all the bees smelling flowers?

1 bee and 9 bees $\xrightarrow{\text{together make}}$ 10 bees

1 and 9 $\xrightarrow{\text{together make}}$ 10

There are many animals
in this picture. Can you find . . .

1 kangaroo

2 mice

3 rabbits

4 elephants

5 zebras

6 lions

All kinds of animals hide
in the jungle.
Can you find hiding in the leaves . . .

7 snakes

8 giraffes

9 birds

10 monkeys

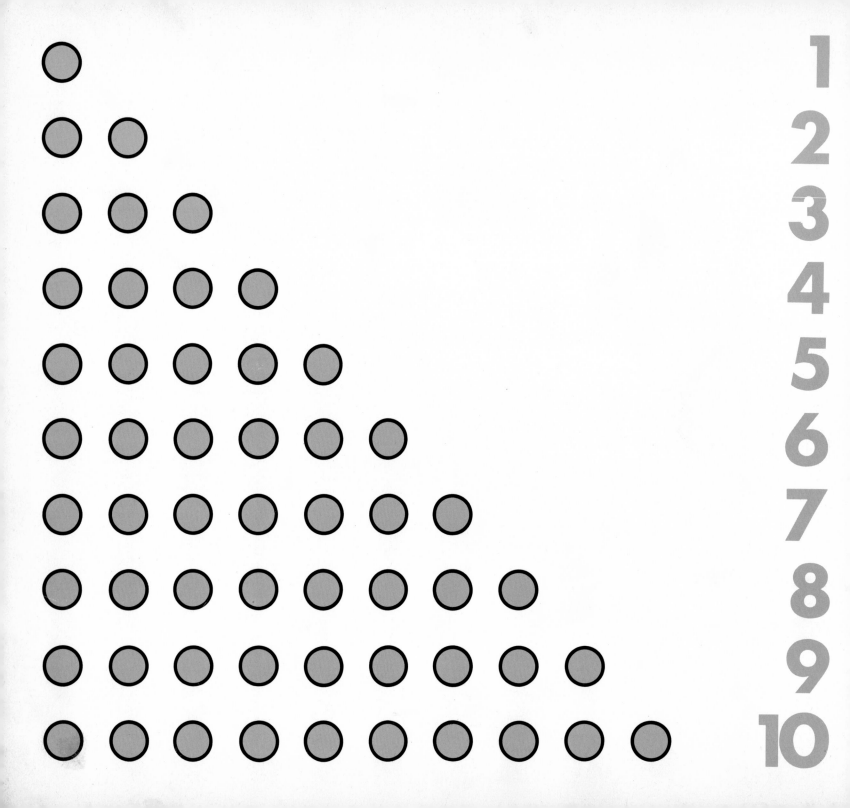